Basic Counselling Skills

A Student Guide

By Kenneth Kelly

Co-Director of CounsellingTutor.com

This book would not have been possible without
the editing skills of Sarah Carr from Carr Consultancy,
and the layout and design skills of Laurice Chavez,
my personal assistant and friend.

ISBN: 978-0-9957696-1-8

Table of Content

Foreword

When Ken Kelly asked me to write a foreword to his book, I was both humbled and delighted in equal measure.

Humbled because what started off as a tutor- student relationship has metamorphosed in to a deep friendship as well as an enduring respect for Ken's dedication to the craft of counselling.

Delighted, as it was clear from the day Ken walked in to my level 3 class on a sunny September afternoon in 2008 that he was serious individual committed to his studies.

Little did I realise that nine years on he would become one of the people who changed the way counsellor education is delivered, not just in the United Kingdom but throughout the world.

Ken's acute understanding of how students learn in the age of the internet has been nothing short of transformational.

Although you may be reading this book in printed form, it's a testament to Ken's forward thinking that you can also access this on your phone, tablet, computer or E-Reader as well as in audio format.

It's not surprising that the topic Ken chose for his first counselling publication would be that of counselling skills. You see, this is his passion, an area of expertise he developed when we taught together at Warrington Collegiate between 2013-2015

'Skills with Ken' may very well be a tag-line for one of our podcast segments. However, like all our good ideas, it came from the students we taught, who gave the name to the skill sessions he delivered, every week during that two-year period.

Recently, I was interviewing the well-known and respected psychotherapist Richard Erskine, for a piece on the integrative psychotherapy conference in Milan. During the course of the interview the subject of being a skilled therapist came up. We both agreed that honing one's skills is essential to effective helping no matter what level or modality you practice at.

Which neatly brings me to the reason why I believe this book is important. One of the overwhelming messages we received from both our students and those we interact with on social media is how to apply counselling skills in a measured way without sounding 'contrived or rehearsed'.

Ken skilfully (see what I did there!) develops not only a theoretical argument for the use of the skill but goes on to contextualise where it would be most effective in the therapeutic interaction.

Add to that examples and audio recordings of Ken applying the skill, and links with counselling theory and I am convinced that it will help you with assignments and more importantly real world interactions with the clients we serve and support.

I thoroughly enjoyed reading my copy of Basic Counselling Skills – A student's guide and I hope you do to.

Rory Lees-Oakes – *Mossley 2017*

An Introduction to Skills

YOUR CLIENT ARRIVES. You exchange a polite hello as you lead her into the therapy room, where you invite her to sit down. You close the door and realise it's just you and her, two strangers sitting in a quiet room.

The journey from two strangers all the way through to a deep and meaningful therapeutic relationship, with the client trusting you enough to share their innermost pain, is paved by your use of counselling skills.

Through effective use of your skills, rapport is built, trust forms, the client feels heard and understood, edge-of-awareness material is brought into focus, irrational beliefs are challenged, and relational depth (Mearns and Cooper, 2005) is reached – which sometimes leads to moments of profound movement for the client.

During your training to become a practising therapist, you will learn about the theory of your chosen modality. You will study ethical requirements, professional considerations, and how the law underpins your practice. Your understanding of these topics will be assessed through assignments that hit certain criteria, set by an awarding body.

Counselling skills are much more difficult to assess effectively. Yes, you will write about the theory of the skill to show you understand what it is and how it is to be used. But measuring the nuance of your skills used within a real counselling relationship is not possible due to the confidential nature of counselling.

Counselling skills are therefore often assessed by a tutor observing a simulated counselling session or listening to a simulated session recording. But a simulated session lacks the relational depth that is often present in a real counselling relationship. Students can become nervous when being observed. They may find that they act differently from how they would when relaxed and integrated in a real therapeutic relationship.

I recognise that counselling skills don't work in isolation; they are most effective when backed by your theoretical model and underpinned by your empathy and way of being. However when the counselling room door closes, it's your skills that will start to build that bridge, the bridge that transforms a meeting of two strangers into a meaningful therapeutic relationship.

In this book, I go beyond offering just a theoretical definition of what a skill is and an explanation of what it does in a counselling relationship. I share a deeper look into the skills and explore a more philosophical explanation from my own experience as a practising therapist and former counselling tutor. The skill is explained and, in some cases, also demonstrated in a simulated session so you can hear how it is used and understand how it influences a session. The audio files can be listened to online, or downloaded and played on any smartphone, tablet, laptop or computer.

In *On Becoming a Person,* Carl Rogers (1961, pp. 23–24): said:

> *Experience is, for me, the highest authority.* The touchstone of validity is my own experience. No other person's ideas, and none of my own ideas, are as authoritative as my experience. It is to experience that I must return again and again, to discover a closer approximation to truth as it is in the process of becoming in me.

Neither the Bible nor the prophets – neither Freud nor research – neither the revelations of God nor man – can take precedence over my own direct experience.

… My experience is not authoritative because it is infallible. It is the basis of authority because it can always be checked in new primary ways. In this way its frequent error or fallibility is always open to correction.

This book is written from my own frame of reference, based on my own understanding and experience. I challenge you to read beyond my words and find your own unique meaning and understanding of the skills based on you as a person. If you get something from this book and you wish to tell me, or if you have any questions, then please email me. I would love to hear from you.

Please send emails to ken@counsellingtutor.com.

Chapter 1

Opening a Session

'TOPPING AND TAILING' A COUNSELLING SESSION is an important skill, which is assessed as part of the advanced skills assignment that trainee counsellors on Level 4 diplomas here in the UK must pass. Of course, it's about how all your counselling skills are used, but a lot of the marks are given to how you start and end your session. I know that this can be challenging: what do you need to say, and how do you do so in a way that is respectful to the client?

What Is 'Topping' a Session?

It's a working agreement – an introduction – where we contract for what's going to happen in this session and how. It's important not to rush it – so it might take ten minutes even for a 30-minute skills session. The working agreement empowers the client, giving them choices within the counselling relationship. Checking the client's understanding as we go, we need to explain:

- what's on offer
- our modality of counselling (e.g. person-centred)
- limitations in confidentiality (dependent on the country and legislation there)
- health and safety
- non-maleficence (see the BACP Ethical Framework)
- time boundaries

How about 'Tailing'?

About five or ten minutes before the end of the session, it's important to let the client know that the time is coming to an end, so they have time to 'pack up'. It allows them to 'change gear' and gives you, as the practitioner, the chance to close everything up before they leave, making sure they're safe to 're-enter the world'.

It can be useful to summarise what has been brought to give the client a 'neat package' that they can go away with, feeling understood because the summary matches their material.

Equally, the summary is an opportunity for the client to say, 'No, it's not like that; it's like this.' This too is great for the counsellor, because it allows you to realign where you are and be fully within the client's frame of reference.

An Example of Opening

Below, you'll find an example of contracting, at the start of a counselling session, with the client's replies removed (for reasons of confidentiality). This isn't intended as a perfect example of how to make the working agreement: more to illustrate you how I myself might go about it. Of course, you will develop your own style, but you will see from this the content it's important to include.

 Go to counsellingtutor.com/audio
to listen to the audio example of this skill

Counsellor: Hello, John, my name is Ken. We're here now. This is the time that, having talked on the phone, we come to spend 30 minutes together. I feel it's important – and respectful to you – to be open about what this is: it's a session that will be evaluated, so whatever you choose to bring today, the chances are that an external moderator may come in and also ask for access to the audio file. That may or may not influence what material you choose to bring here today.

I've taken the liberty of putting together a short counselling contract specifically for this session, which I'd like to share with you. So here's a copy for you, and you're more than welcome to take that away and have a look through it. Are you happy for me to go over some of the points?

What I'm really interested in is how the points feel for you. We'll start off with what's on offer, and that's only one session here today. But I think it's also important to realise that if something came up for you in this one session that you felt you might like to explore more deeply, there might be the opportunity for me to refer you on to the college counsellor.

What I offer you for this one session is person-centred counselling. My understanding of this is that together, we 'walk through' whatever you choose to bring. Wherever you choose to lead, I will go with you, and we'll go through it together; it's about you finding the solutions. How does that feel for you?

To touch on health and safety, there are no planned fire drills that I'm aware of, so if there is a fire alarm, that would indicate there may be an emergency. What I would suggest in that instance is that we go together; just follow me and we'll find a safe place.

The session of counselling that we're offering here today is 30 minutes in length, as I mentioned. You can choose to bring whatever you'd like, and we'll explore this in a safe environment.

I think it's important now to speak about confidentiality. We've already covered that this is a recording, and I need us to speak about ownership of that recording. Because of the nature of what it's being used for, I will need to retain that ownership; it'll be loaded onto the VLE [virtual learning environment] as discussed. I feel it's important to make clear that the evaluation of the material in the recording will be about how I am working with you, not about what you're bringing.

I aim to practise ethically, in line with the Ethical Framework of the British Association for Counselling and Psychotherapy.

With confidentiality, there is a legal requirement and an ethical obligation for me to break confidentiality in three instances, and I'd like to go over those now. In all three of these instances, I wouldn't be required to check out with you first. The first is money laundering, so that if you mention that you're involved in or even have any knowledge of money laundering, I would be obliged to break confidentiality. Second, if you were to indicate that you have knowledge of – or were involved in – an act of terrorism, then I would be obliged to break confidentiality. The third is drugs running. That's not the taking of drugs, but drugs running. I wonder: what is your understanding of that term?

You're 100% right. It refers to being involved in the distribution chain for drugs at some point. So are those limits to confidentiality OK with you?

I have regular supervision. As a student counsellor, I have one and a half hours of supervision for every eight hours of face-to-face client contact. There may be elements of this session that I may take into my supervisor. To give you an idea of how I might do this, your name would not be mentioned. I don't give my clients' names at supervision.

Instead, I might say: 'The client brought ...' And again, it's about how I deal with the material. Supervision is a safety net. If I was to miss something really important, I hope that my supervisor would be another set of eyes and ears that might pick up on that. And if my supervisor missed that, well then my supervisor has a supervisor, and so that goes on down the line – and hopefully somebody might pick that up somewhere along the line. It's about best practice and giving you the best service. Is that OK with you?

Regarding notes, I do keep confidential notes from my sessions. However, they are kept in what's called a 'split' filing system. What that means is that any notes are non-descript – by that, I mean there are no distinguishing features that would relate them back to you. Your name is not on them; they would refer simply to 'the client'. I can give you an example of that; would that be helpful for you?

An example might be: 'I was working with the client. The client appeared to be very distressed as the client was crying.' So it would very generic. There would be no distinguishing information that would link you to that or any kind of notes of who you were, and your details would be kept separately. I guess that would be important if my office was broken into, so that you can feel secure there is no personal information that might get out there.

It's also important for you to know who might have access to these notes. I have access to them, and I use that to review where we might be up to in sessions. Also, there are aspects from my notes that I may – as I've mentioned – take to supervision, although I wouldn't take the physical notes, just some information from them. You could have access to the notes, because they're your material. The notes can also be accessed by a subpoena from a court of law, i.e. a court order. And they can be accessed by the coroner, but only with good reason. If somebody ever did request your notes, I would probably try to suggest to them that I did a summary of what had happened in our sessions, as opposed to handing over the actual notes themselves.

That's a lot, and that's why I wanted to give you a printed copy of our agreement, which you can take away, have a look through, and decide about.

Now, how are you feeling with all that? Are you OK? We now have around 20 minutes, and that's your time to bring whatever you may feel comfortable to bring today.

Being Assessed

In episode 4 of the Counselling Tutor Podcast, you can download an example extract from an assignment on opening a counselling session. I hope this will be useful when you're working on your own assignments.

If I was asked for one tip on having your skills assessed, I would say: tell it as it is. In other words, if there's somebody sitting there with a pad and a pen marking your skill session, don't be shy to say to your 'client': 'Hey, here's how it is. Somebody is sitting there writing. I see that; you see that.' Don't pretend they're not there – or, if you're recording the session, that the recording device isn't there – because that would mean the congruence was gone from the relationship.

> **"**
>
> **The core conditions are both necessary and sufficient to bring about an environment where a client can move from rigidity to fluidity.**
>
> **"**

As a person-centred counsellor, I look to Carl Rogers, who said that the core conditions are both necessary and sufficient to bring about an environment where a client can move from rigidity to fluidity.

Chapter 2
Rapport-Building

RAPPORT-BUILDING IS THE BEDROCK OF WHAT WE OFFER as counsellors and psychotherapists. We begin to look at this right from the start, in Level 2 training (the introduction to counselling), and we continue to write about it right up to when we submit our final portfolio. Even in a counselling dissertation, rapport-building will be mentioned, because it 'knits' its way through what we offer as counsellors.

What Is Rapport?

Rapport is the way we are within the relationship, letting the client know that we are:

- there for them
- listening to them
- attentive and focused on what they are bringing
- looking from their frame of reference rather than our own.

Rapport-building is important no matter what modality of counselling we're practising – because if the client doesn't feel a sense that we are there for and with them, they will be unlikely to feel enough trust to bring any heavy material to the counselling relationship.

So a definition of rapport might be 'a sense of having a connection with the client, and the client sensing that very same connection'. As the second part of that definition suggests, rapport is not something simply that the counsellor demonstrates: it is built within the relationship, and so is present between the counsellor and the client.

A Way of Being

I believe that rapport is less something we do than something we are. Carl Rogers spoke of 'a way of being' – it's about how we present ourselves from the very moment the client meets us to the very last session when they go on their way.

It can be tempting, in a recorded skill session that is going to be evaluated, to try to 'switch on' the rapport. But for me, that feels false and incongruent. I believe that the very essence of rapport is being our true selves, taking ourselves – just as we are – into that relationship. So we're not there in the session trying to be the counsellor; we are just being ourselves, receptive to what that client is bringing.

However, there are things that we can do as counsellors to prepare to demonstrate that rapport.

Importance of Preparing

First, being well-prepared for the session is important. This means being ready to enter the session in a calm, unrushed way so that we can be present for the client. We can maybe take the opportunity to spend five or ten minutes grounding ourselves and being present before the client arrives, perhaps also looking over our notes and/or thinking back to our last sessions with this client. As the client arrives, we will in essence already be with them. Conversely, if – two minutes before the client walks in – we're seeing to our emails, we're unlikely to be in the right mindset to be fully there.

The Counselling Environment

Another way that we can encourage rapport is to look at the counselling environment itself, making sure that it is safe and uncluttered. It is very important that the client feels that what they are bringing will be treated as confidential – that it can't be overheard through a non-soundproof wall, or seen through an unscreened window.

Remembering Key Information

As a counsellor, it's important to remember the names of the client and the people they talk about, and the key issues from previous sessions. This is information that we can remind ourselves of when reading through the client's notes in preparation for the forthcoming session. This all goes towards building rapport – showing the client that we care, are paying attention and are there with them.

Mirroring

Mirroring is another great way to build rapport. By this, I mean looking at the client, how they are sitting and how they present themselves within the relationship, and demonstrating – perhaps with our tone of voice – our response to what they are bringing.

> **"**
>
> **Rapport-building is important ... because if the client doesn't feel a sense that we are there for and with them, they will be unlikely to feel enough trust to bring any heavy material to the counselling relationship.**
>
> **"**

The pace of the counselling session is also important here: if the client is speaking slowly and being really considered in what they bring, we can mirror that back in speaking slowly. Conversely, it would be a mismatch if we quickly rattled off, in a summary, what the client had said.

It is also good to mirror the weight of the material that is being brought. If the material is particularly deep and meaningful to the client, then we can show our understanding by respecting that act of great trust.

The Core Conditions

Last but by no means least, the core conditions of empathy, unconditional positive regard (UPR) and congruence are vital ingredients in building rapport. Empathy involves seeing things from the client's perspective, and responding in such a way that the client feels that they have been understood: the circle of empathy is then complete. UPR is about seeing the client for who they are, recognising them without judgement as a fellow human being, and so being there for them no matter what they bring – however deep, dark and scary. And congruence is about being fully integrated – being who we really are – within that relationship.

Together, the core conditions build deep rapport and trust within the relationship. And with deep rapport and trust, we are able to work at relational depth (Mearns and Cooper, 2005) – which is where real movement happens.

Next Steps in Rapport-Building

Have a think about what rapport-building means for you. Think about your own life and relationships. Are there certain people that you just get along well with? If so, what is it within those relationships that makes them work? Think too about the people that you feel less comfortable with: what do you see in terms of rapport within those relationships? Where does that sense of discomfort come from?

Chapter 3

The Skill of Silence

I RECOGNISE THAT SILENCE CAN FEEL UNCOMFORTABLE, heavy and really unnatural. If we look to our culture, that's no wonder: it's common to hear people talking about 'uncomfortable' or 'awkward' silences, even when with good friends. Suddenly, nobody knows what to say, and both people's minds are whirring, trying to find words to fill that silence.

But we're not talking here about silence during a conversation with a friend; we're talking about silence as a skill in a counselling setting – within a therapeutic relationship, and for the sole benefit of the client's movement and journey. This is a very different kind of silence. It's a silence that we need to understand and to practise.

Learning to Love Silence

When I mention silence to my beginner learners, who are just starting their journey into counselling, and set them the task of discussing in small groups what silence means for them and how they think it is appropriate in a counselling relationship, I rarely get more than five to ten minutes of feedback. But interestingly, when I give that same topic to my diploma learners, who are now approaching qualification as counsellors, we can happily sit and speak for an hour or more on the power of silence. This is because, by now, they've been in practice and they've experienced the real power of silence within their placements; they've seen how silence benefits clients and the therapeutic relationship.

What is Silence?

Let's start off with a textbook definition of what silence is; this type of definition is what you need in an academic assignment where you have to describe silence. Feltham and Dryden (1993, p. 177) define silence within counselling as 'the temporary absence of any overt verbal or paraverbal communication between counsellor and client within sessions'.

But what really is silence? What happens when you take silence into a counselling relationship? How can silence make a difference in a client's journey?

How Silence Helps Counsellors

- Silence encourages the client to explore themselves and reinforces what person-centred counselling is all about. So a client might look to us, and we would use silence to reflect that back, in effect saying: 'No, you look. You look yourself. I'm not the expert. I'm not here to guide you and give you advice. This lies with you.' For me, this links clearly to unconditional positive regard, to trusting that the client will find their own way. So if they look at me expectantly, I might use silence, with a warm, accepting smile. The body language used by the counsellor within that silence makes all the difference.

- Silence gives the client autonomy within the session, so that they set the pace for the counselling. If we jumped in and asked a question, we would be setting the tempo of the counselling session, or leading the client somewhere else.

- Silence can enable you as counsellor to collect your thoughts and feelings, to process what the client is saying. There are times where the client will bring something and I, as the counsellor, really do need a moment or two to understand what that is, to be with them. So, silence is a great place to do that. If I immediately launch into the skill of reflection or paraphrasing, am I allowing myself as the counsellor to fully absorb what it is that client has shared?

- The counsellor can use silence as a natural ending to a discussion, to some material that the client has brought. Maybe the client has reached a natural end on that, and wishes to go somewhere else now; a little bit of silence is almost like a gear change, allowing the client the space to head off and pick up new material.

How Silence Helps Clients

- Silence gives the client time to make connections – to find the words, images or feelings they are looking for. Remember that this may be the first time – especially for a client new to counselling – that they're really putting names to feelings. For them, it may be a knot in their stomach or a tightness in their chest, and now they're trying to find the words to describe that. Silence gives them the time to really look and find the words, so they can share that with you as their counsellor.

- Silence can provide a space where feelings can be nurtured and allowed to develop. For me, this is about process – so important in counselling. The client brings material, shares this with us, and we look at it together. Through processing the material, the client moves from rigidity to fluidity, experiencing an organismic shift and so a moment of movement. No process ever happens when words are being spoken: words may lead to the process, but the process itself happens only in silence.

- It may well be that the weight of the material that is being brought is emotionally heavy: tears are streaming down the face of the client as they feel the pain, which – previously suppressed – is right there in the room in the here-and-now. Silence allows the space for those emotions to be felt fully and processed.

- Just as we as counsellors sometimes need a little silence to collect our thoughts, and to be completely with the material that is going on, the same is true for the client. Silence gives the client time to 'get everything in order'.

Tones of Silence

We speak about different tones of voice, different tones in language, but silence has different tones as well. Silence is not about just being there and being quiet. Silence is about being 100% present with the client within that silence. We 'listen' to the silence – just as we listen to the client's verbal communication. Much of our communication as human beings is wordless; it's about body language. So when silence

> "
> A client might look to us, and we would use silence to reflect that back, in effect saying: 'No, you look. You look yourself. I'm not the expert. I'm not here to guide you and give you advice. This lies with you.'
> "

arrives within the counselling relationship, communication hasn't stopped. Communication continues.

For example, have you ever been in an argument with a loved one where you stop talking to one another, or where one person is trying to restart conversation and you're not answering? Think of the power and the message that is being broadcast in that non-verbal communication. It can be just as powerful and meaningful as words.

Using Silence Appropriately

However, don't forget that silence must be used appropriately. Silence can sometimes feel uncomfortable and embarrassing for the right reasons. For example, Carl Rogers (1942, p. 165) said: 'In an initial interview, long pauses or silence are likely to be embarrassing rather than helpful. In subsequent contacts, however, if fundamental rapport is good, silence on the part of the counselor may be a most useful device.'

So even Rogers says that it's OK for silence to feel uncomfortable at times, because it's an effective tool only when used appropriately. To achieve this, you need relational depth (Mearns and Cooper, 2005) – in other words, to have built really good rapport with the client.

Getting Comfortable with Silence

As I have shown, we need to allow silence as counsellors. We can do this only if we practise doing so. I implore you to take silence into your next skills session and to work on it really hard. Practise it, hone it, and watch the power of silence unfold.

I could write much more about silence: I love it! I think it is an incredibly powerful skill. Yet I know it to be an underused skill, because of what it brings up for us as therapists. But remember that this whole journey of becoming – and then of being – a counsellor, is about us exploring self and the things we struggle with.

Chapter 4

Reflection

REFLECTION IS LIKE HOLDING UP A MIRROR: repeating the client's words back to them exactly as they said them. You might reflect back the whole sentence, or you might select a few words – or even one single word – from what the client has brought.

I often refer to reflection as 'the lost skill' because when I watch learners doing simulated skill sessions, or listen to their recordings from placement (where clients have consented to this), I seldom see it being used. This is a pity, as reflection can be very powerful.

When we use reflection, we are looking to match the tone, the feeling of the words, and the client's facial expression or body language as they spoke. For example, they might have hunched their shoulders as they said, 'I was so scared; I didn't know what to do.' We might reflect that back by hunching our own shoulders, mirroring their body language, while also saying 'I felt so scared; I didn't know what to do.'

So why do we use reflection? Is it an effective skill? What does it do within the therapeutic relationship?

Enabling the Client to Feel Heard

First – and really importantly – the client feels heard. And we are reflecting back only their agenda; we are not putting our agenda in there at all. That is true unconditional positive regard – respecting that the client will set the pace of their journey and ensuring they feel heard build rapport, which in turn deepens trust within the therapeutic relationship.

Giving a New Perspective

Interestingly, the client may hear the words as if for the very first time. When the client has a narrative going around in their head, it's almost going in a circular motion. But as soon as they share this with you in a session, it changes direction: it is now out, so it is linear. And when you take that and reflect it back – almost like hitting back a tennis ball – the client's own words can sometimes be quite surprising to them. This allows the client to process and sometimes even clarify their words.

For example, the client may be struggling with a relationship issue, and may say: 'I am really struggling to get on with him in the relationship. He is always bringing me down.' Your reflection here might be: 'He's always bringing me down.' There may be a slight pause as the client hears their very own words back, and it may be that they look quizzically and say, 'No, well. No, he's not really. He is not always bringing me down; we do have our good times,' and then carry on with the narrative.

> "
>
> **When the client has a narrative going around in their head, it's almost going in a circular motion. But as soon as they share this with you in a session, it changes direction: it is now out, so it is linear. And when you take that and reflect it back … the client's own words can sometimes be quite surprising to them.**
>
> "

Focusing Down

Reflection can also be used to focus down – that is, almost to 'cut through' the narrative and to drill right down to the feelings. You may well have seen this in your practice, placement or simulated skill sessions. When a client brings heavy, painful material, it is often really difficult for them to go down to the feelings. So they tell the story and, every now and again, they'll dip down and touch on those feelings. As they feel that pain, they may quickly run away from those feelings back into the relative safety of the narrative. We can reflect back the feelings words – just those few words that the client said that touched on the feeling.

For example, a client might say: 'You know, I'm trying as hard as I can, but it's really killing me. But I go in to work and I try to be strong, and I just carry on.' And we can reflect back and say: 'It's really killing me.' This invites the client to go back and look at that, because that is the feeling. That is the 'meat' of what they are bringing; the rest is the narrative that is wrapped around that. And if you reflect feelings in a relationship where rapport is built and the empathy levels are deep, the client may accept that invitation, go back and say: 'Yes, it is. I just feel that I can't go on anymore. I'm so devastated; I feel so much pain.' And they are there then – out of the narrative and fully in the emotions of what it is that they are bringing.

Clarifying Our Understanding

We can also use reflection to clarify our understanding, instead of a question. For example, suppose the client says: 'My husband and my father are fighting. I'm really angry with him.' For me to be in the client's frame of reference, I need to know whether 'him' refers to the husband or the father. So I might reflect back the word 'him', with a quizzical look. The client might then respond: 'Yeah, my dad. He really gets to me when he is non-accepting.' So you can get clarification in this way, so you can adjust where you are to make sure that the empathic bond is strong and that you are truly within that client's frame of reference.

An Example

Let's look now at a simulated skill session where reflection is used:

 Go to counsellingtutor.com/audio
to listen to the audio example of this skill

Client:	And as I sort of reflect and look over that kind of situation; so often, I would sacrifice my own wants and my own desires. If there was nobody else involved in the situation, what I would choose to do would be very different from what I actually end up doing.
Counsellor:	Sacrifice my own wants?
Client:	[Moment of silence] Yeah. It really feels like putting aside what I would do out of my own free choice and favouring what would be the accepted thing or – in my perception – what I think someone else would rather I do.

Here, the counsellor reflects the feeling that seems to underlie what the client is bringing. It is interesting that the reflection causes a moment of silence for the client, who is mindfully looking at that.

In this session, the narrative continued in a very feeling way, where the client took that invitation and decided to go and explore the feelings more deeply. Later in the same session, there's another use of reflection:

Client: The thought of doing or maybe expressing my wants and what I would like to do that feels very selfish ... for some reason, it feels like: but why put my own wants and needs in front of what someone else might choose?

Counsellor: Why put my own wants and needs in front of what somebody else might choose?

Client: [Pause] Yeah. I guess, I don't know what they'd choose, so the only thing I can do is I guess, or ask. But also look after myself.

Here, the reflection was a question that came up in the narrative that the client was bringing: 'Why put my own wants and needs in front of what somebody else might choose?' In hearing that back, it's like the client is hearing that for the first time, differently. And that is evident by the pause that is there, while the client reflects – as a result of the counsellor's reflection. And the client then answers that for herself; there has been a small moment of movement, which can be heard in the answering of that question.

Next Steps in Reflection

Try using the skill of reflection in your simulated skill sessions within your learning environment. If possible, contract with the person you're working with to record your sessions (you don't need special technology – your smartphone will do), listen back, and hear the power of reflection. Carl Rogers was recording sessions really early on, when recording equipment was relatively new. He reflected that his greatest learning came from these recordings.

Let's try together to make reflection not the lost skill that is seldom heard, but a powerful skill that enables our clients to move on, to process, and to become more fully functioning people!

Chapter 5
Paraphrasing

PARAPHRASING IS REPEATING BACK YOUR UNDERSTANDING of the material that has been brought by the client, using your own words. A paraphrase reflects the essence of what has been said.

We all use paraphrasing in our everyday lives. If you look at your studies to become a counsellor or psychotherapist, you paraphrase in class. Maybe your lecturer brings a body of work, and you listen and make notes: you're paraphrasing, as you distil this down to what you feel is important.

How Paraphrasing Builds Empathy

How does paraphrasing affect the client–counsellor relationship? First of all, it helps the client to feel both heard and understood. The client brings their material, daring to share that with you. And you show that you're listening by giving them a little portion of that back – the part that feels the most important. You paraphrase it down. And if you do that accurately and correctly, and it matches where the client is, the client is going to recognise that and feel heard: 'Finally, somebody is there really listening, really understanding what it is that I am bringing.'

This keys right into empathy, because it's about building that empathic relationship with the client. And empathy is not a one-way transaction. Carl Rogers (1959, pp. 210–211) defines 'empathy' as the ability to 'perceive the internal frame of reference of another with accuracy and with the emotional components and meanings which pertain thereto as if one were the person, but without ever losing the "as if" conditions'. In other words, we walk in somebody's shoes as if their reality is our reality – but of course it's not our reality, and that's where the 'as if' comes in. I've heard this rather aptly described as 'walking in the client's shoes, but keeping our socks on'!

Empathy is a two-way transaction – that is, it's not enough for us to be 100% in the client's frame of reference, understanding their true feelings; the client must also perceive that we understand. When the client feels at some level that they have been understood, then the empathy circle is complete.

For example, if you watch a TV programme in which somebody achieves something that is really spectacular, you may find yourself moved for this person. You're almost there with them on this journey, and as they're receiving their award or their adulation, and the audience is clapping for what they've done, you may even be moved to tears. But the person on the TV cannot perceive your reaction – the empathy is empty, because it's one-way.

So empathy is effective only if your client feels heard and understood – i.e. they sense that empathic connection. Using paraphrasing is a way of completing the empathy circle – a way of letting them know that we see and hear them.

> **"**
>
> **Empathy is a two-way transaction – that is, it's not enough for us to be 100% in the client's frame of reference, understanding their true feelings; the client must also perceive that we understand.**
>
> **"**

Other Benefits of Paraphrasing

Paraphrasing also highlights issues by stating them more concisely. This is focusing down: it invites the client to go and delve deeper into part of what they have said. We can also use paraphrasing to check out the accuracy of our perception as a counsellor.

The following is an example of my use of paraphrasing to clarify my understanding of what was brought up. This shows how paraphrasing affects the therapeutic relationship; because the paraphrase fits well for the client, she feels heard and understood. As this happens, the material deepens.

 Go to counsellingtutor.com/audio
to listen to the audio example of this skill

Client: I really have a battle with doing things for the impression that others will have of me, or the approval that I will get from other people for what it is that I do. So much so that I will very often override myself, my family, so that I can gain the acceptance, I guess, of other people, whether friends, family or clients in a work situation. I will always favour what the action would be that would gain that acceptance, that would not bring up any sort of confrontation or maybe have a conflict situation arise from it.

So, I guess, I'm eager to please, wanting to make sure that all things are well and smooth – and that I'm liked and accepted with whatever the transaction or situation may be.

Counsellor: As you're saying that, it really feels like a lot of hard work. A lot of hard work, and pre-empting whatever it is that they would have expected of you. And then 'sacrificing', I guess, is a word that came up for me – sacrificing your own wants/needs to be able to meet what you perceive is expected of you. Have I understood that correctly?

Client: Yeah, the word 'sacrifice' really captures the feeling that comes up for me when I sort of reflect and look over that kind of situation. So often, I will sacrifice my own wants and my own desire ...

In this example, the client really resonated with the word 'sacrifice', which the counsellor introduced as a paraphrase; she really felt understood. And it's interesting to note that throughout the rest of this simulated session, the word 'sacrifice' became almost a theme.

Another paraphrase in this example was 'hard work'. Although the client hadn't used this phrase herself, she was presenting visually as weighed down. Her shoulders looked heavy as she was bringing the material. So the counsellor was paraphrasing, not only the words of the narrative, but digging deeper, looking for the feelings and paraphrasing the whole presence of that client within that relationship.

Listening for 'the Music behind the Words'

Here is another example of paraphrasing, from the same skills session. Try to see if you can hear, as Rogers would put it, 'the music behind the words', where the counsellor looks deeper than just the words the client is bringing, paraphrasing back their whole being.

Client:	Out of my own will or my own free choice, I would put that aside and favour what would be accepted – or what I think someone else would rather I do. And sometimes it's hard. It leaves me with a situation of not knowing if they actually really realise what it is that I sacrificed, that I've given up, so that it can fall into what I think they would prefer in that situation.
Counsellor:	It feels confusing to you in that situation of whether they even perceive what it is that you are sacrificing, what you're giving up. That it almost feels like you're giving up part of yourself to match what you think they may want or need from you. And I kind of got the feeling, as you were saying it, that you wonder if they even see that.
Client:	Yeah. As I was sort of verbalising and talking through that, I actually realised that even within that sacrifice, it's all my perception of what I think they might want me to do. And just saying that is actually a bit ridiculous. Because how am I to know what it is that they want or need to do? So here I am – disregarding my own desires, for lack of a better word – to do something I assume someone else would want me to do instead.

I thought it was really interesting that this client started off in what felt to me like an external locus of evaluation. She was confused, and wondering whether the people she refers to understood what she was giving up to meet their perceived expectations.

Immediately after the counsellor's paraphrase, this client experienced a moment of movement from an external to an internal locus of evaluation, where she realised it was all about her own perceptions and responsibility. In this way, she went from being powerless to having the power to change this situation.

Next Steps in Paraphrasing

Paraphrasing is so much more than just repeating the client's words back to them using your own words. Although it might feel very simplistic – and there's often a tendency to paraphrase the narrative/story that the client brings, rather than their feelings/process – there's so much more to it than that. There's so much deeper that we can go. There's real power in paraphrasing.

I suggest that you:

- practise paraphrasing in your own simulated skills sessions
- try to look for the full person when paraphrasing, e.g. not just the client's words, but also their body language, facial expressions, and way of being within the counselling relationship
- record these sessions (with your peer's consent) and listen back to them
- speak to your peers about paraphrasing
- evaluate each other's paraphrasing

- look whether you're getting empathic connection within your paraphrasing
- search out moments of movement when you paraphrase
- ask how paraphrasing affects both the client and you, as a counsellor.

Paraphrasing is definitely something that should be debated. I hope that this chapter will encourage you to go out there with a new passion for – and a new way of looking at – paraphrasing!

Chapter 6

Focusing

FOCUSING IS SOMETIMES MISUNDERSTOOD as a term, quite understandably. Because when we think about the word 'focusing', we may be drawn to thinking that it's about us paying more attention and really focusing our concentration on something that the client is bringing. But it's not this at all. Focusing is listening to what the client is bringing, and then choosing an area to focus on, pushing the rest of it aside for now so we lead or invite the client to explore in more depth the area where we feel the focus should be.

Choosing Where to Focus

So where do we focus client attention in this way? One of the places we might choose is if the client brings a feeling word. It often happens in counselling that the client will come in with a story. Although they bring in the weight of this material, there is also an element of safety in staying in the story, because there's a distance between this and feelings that underlie this. Some of these feelings may be really painful. And that's our work as counsellors: to be there in those painful feelings with people.

How to Focus

But how do we then focus down on that? Do we stop them and say, 'Hold on; let's talk about that'? My approach to counselling is person-centred – which is, by nature, non-directive. There are different approaches where the counsellor may be more directive and more solution-based – but in person-centred counselling, we would need to invite the client to explore something. How might we do this?

 Go to counsellingtutor.com/audio to listen to the audio example of this skill

First of all, we need to be in their frame of reference. The client is bringing their story. Maybe they will touch on a feeling word as they're going through that story. And as a person-centred counsellor, I might just use a really simple reflection of the feeling word that they brought. That would be me acknowledging that the feeling is there – and inviting the client (if they choose and feel ready to do so) to go to that feeling and to focus on it, drilling down to bring more of themselves. Here's an example:

Counsellor: But when it comes to making that choice of doing something for self, you use the word 'selfish'.

Client: Very much so. It feels – when it is for my own gain, want or pleasing – I guess, it really feels selfish.

So in this example, the focus word is 'selfish'. That's because when the story was brought, the word 'selfish' didn't seem to fit for the client; she didn't seem to resonate with it, and it seemed to be a pain area. So I purposely reflected that word back. It was her word that she brought, and it was an invitation to focus down on what 'selfish' meant to her, allowing the client to explore that.

So look out, among all the material that the client brings, for when a client uses a 'feeling' word. That's a great place to go back and focus down on. It's like the client is taking a flag, bashing it into the material that they're bringing, and saying, 'Look, there's a feeling that lives under here!' It may well be that the client chooses not to take up that invitation and so not to look at that feeling right now, and that's OK. At least you have acknowledged that by focusing, and that in itself lets the client know that they've been understood.

Moments of Movement

Another place where we can use focusing is if there has been a moment of movement within the counselling session. If the client has experienced some development or growth – no matter how small that is – that may be a massive win for the client. So let's celebrate that. We're not there just to dig and find pain, and take the clients to the places that are uncomfortable for them. We can also focus on something that the client feels is a small moment of movement; we can acknowledge that and say, 'Yes. Wow, look at that!' Here's an example of this type of focusing:

Client: Not to assume what the other person would like, need or want from that, but to allow them maybe to express that, to bring what it is that I would do and maybe not be so sensitive if it's not taken up or accepted, and to allow for whatever the situation is that occurs, that it's not a rejection of me. It's just ...

Counsellor: It's not a rejection of me.

Client: Yeah, it's just a choice or a decision or a like or a want or whatever, but it's not ultimately rejecting me.

Counsellor: Wow.

Client: Just the thought or the ...

Counsellor: That feels massive. That really feels massive when you say, 'Not a rejection of me,' because mere moments ago, you were talking about that as being a rejection. It feels like, looking at it and examining it, you may be able to see that slightly different now. You're acknowledging that not as a rejection of you and, I guess, as maybe their opinion, want or need. But at the same time, I recognise how fragile that want and need of self is, feeling that it does take second place. So I guess it's about maybe that courage to bring your wants and needs out, measured against the idea that 'it's not a rejection of me'.

Client: Yeah. It doesn't feel as make or break, or life and death anymore. The idea of me purely expressing something that I'd prefer is not the ultimate 'this is going to be you liking me or not liking me'. It's purely a thought or an idea.

Just hearing those words that it's not so 'life and death' anymore really warms me. It's just amazing, and it's what counselling is all about. It's a massive moment of movement. Only moments before, the client was speaking about how she felt judged and evaluated by other people when she was making decisions for herself. And now, thanks to a little focus on that moment of movement, it doesn't feel like that anymore for her. She's able to see that there is a change.

Next Steps

So focusing is a very useful and necessary skill in what we do as counsellors. I challenge you to practise focusing. You can use various different techniques to focus, for example a one-word reflection or a paraphrase. Why not try sharing with peers what it feels like for you to invite somebody to focus down on something? Focusing can encourage a client – if they wish – to go and explore a feeling or movement more deeply. This deepens the bond, taking the therapeutic connection to a new relational depth (Mearns and Cooper, 2005). I hope you'll go out there and look at the skill of focusing with new focus!

> **We're not there just to dig and find pain, and take the clients to the places that are uncomfortable for them. We can also focus on something that the client feels is a small moment of movement.**

Chapter 7

Appropriate Questioning

IN THE TERM 'APPROPRIATE QUESTIONING', the word 'appropriate' is really important. That's because so often, questions are inappropriate – and this can derail the empathy within the counselling relationship. Appropriate questioning, meanwhile, can deepen relational depth (Mearns and Cooper, 2005) with the client.

The use of questions is usually covered quite early on in counselling training – I do so with my Level 2 learners (in the introduction to counselling, Counselling Concepts). As well as introducing the theory that I cover here, I warn them that questioning is to be used only when 100% necessary. And very often, questions are not necessary.

Questioning in Person-Centred Counselling

I am working from a person-centred base here. So it may well be that, in other modalities, questions that delve into, explore and expand on elements of the narrative that the client is bringing are encouraged and are appropriate. But in the person-centred approach, we believe that the client is the expert; this is what Carl Rogers told us. It's not for us to guide the client. It's for the client to guide us, and for us to walk with them in their subjective reality. That is the empathic bond that we have with the client.

If we ask a question, it is for our knowledge – for us to better understand what the client is bringing. We must be really careful that our questions don't set the agenda – that we are allowing the client to do this, even when (and this can be difficult) we can see that the meat of what the client needs to work on is in a different direction. We might feel we can see it: it's there, it's massive, and the client is so close to it – they just need a tiny nudge and then they'll see it. So if we ask the right question, the client is suddenly going to see this massive mound of opportunity for them to grow. But this is not our journey; it's the client's journey. It's for them to find the mound of opportunity, and it may well not be the same one that we see.

 Go to counsellingtutor.com/audio to listen to the audio example of this skill

Cognition or Emotion?

Also, questions are cognitive; in other words, you answer a question not from your emotional core but from looking around in your head. You cognitively search for the answer, you find it, and then you bring that information out to the person who has asked the question. But within counselling, we're looking to touch on emotion. We're looking to submerge ourselves in the emotion – the pain, the distress, the discomfort. We recognise that it's a difficult journey for the client, and we're there with them (no matter how scary that may be) so they don't have to go alone. If we ask a question, we take the client straight out of that emotional bath of richness and put them right into their head, where they cognitively search for the answer. It's like there's a disconnect from the emotion when we answer a question.

You can hear this in action by listening to recorded skill sessions. Listen to where the client is before you ask the question, and the kind of words they're using. And then look at where they are afterwards: has it dragged the client away from the feeling? Very often, it has.

Rogers' View of Questioning

Rogers reckons that we don't need to ask questions, other than to clarify our understanding. I think this is pure genius; my admiration for Rogers increases the more I study his work. If we are to have that empathic bond – and empathy means being there within the client's frame of reference – then we need to know that we've got that frame of reference correct. And if we're not sure, we need to clarify. The way we do that is to ask a question.

When we ask a question in that situation, we're not bringing in our agenda in; we're just trying hard to be in the frame of reference of the client, and so we reflect their words within the question. Here's an example of where a question is used to clarify:

Client: It feels – when it is for my own gain, want or pleasing – I guess, it really feels selfish.

Counsellor: I wonder if I can check with you, just so that I can fully understand the word 'selfish' as you see it and feel it. What does 'selfish' mean to you?

Client: My interpretation of it is very much for self-gain and self-pleasure, I guess – wanting my own way, and in a context, where, maybe in a family situation, choices arise and all that. If I was to push my own wishes or my wants, it just feels so closed off, not being able to incorporate all. Going through this, I guess the expression of what I would want and need doesn't ultimately mean that this is what's going to end up happening. However, I feel that, if I was to express my own wants and needs, I would somehow be insisting that it follows what I want and need. And that's not always, I guess, true in every situation. Maybe, sometimes, and then maybe not. But the fear, I guess, is that someone else not having their want and need mentioned or met in exchange for mine, it feels like an unfair trade. I don't know. I would rather it be someone else's wishes, and I'd go along with theirs. And I don't know where that comes from.

When the client answers my question, she's initially moved from being in an emotional to in a cognitive place. But then the question – used for clarification – actually deepens where the client goes, and she starts using a lot more feeling words. Because the question is about keeping in her frame of reference, it doesn't take very long before she uses the words 'I feel' again, and she deeply explores the word 'selfish'.

Open versus Closed Questions

There are two types of questions in counselling. Closed questions have a 'yes' or 'no' answer; these should be avoided, as they kind of stop everything dead. Instead, we need to use open questions; these ask the client to elaborate on or clarify something. For example, the client could not answer just 'yes' or 'no' to the question in the dialogue above; it requires her to clarify – to delve deeper.

Alternatives to Questions

What else can we use when we're not sure what exactly a client means? For example, if a client was speaking about his brother and father, he might say: 'I really struggle with my brother and my father. They don't get on, and at times he makes me so angry.' Who does the client mean by 'he': the brother or the father? Not knowing who makes him angry means I cannot be fully within the client's frame of reference.

> **" But this is not our journey; it's the client's journey. It's for them to find the mound of opportunity, and it may well not be the same one that we see. "**

I could ask: 'Sorry, just so I can understand, who is it that you're angry at – your father or your brother?' This risks ripping the client out of that emotion (the anger). Instead, we could use reflection: 'He makes you so angry.' This invites the client to expand on what he has said. He might say: 'Yes, ever since I was a young boy, my dad was always ...' In this case, I didn't need to ask a question – we're still in the feelings, and I've got what I needed in order to be fully in the client's frame of reference.

Of course, the client might not reveal the information I need in his answer – for example, if he responded to my reflection: 'He does. He makes me really angry – in fact, so angry that I don't know what to do about it anymore.' In that case, I would still need to put in a question: ''Is this your dad or your brother that you're referring to?'

How about You?

So this chapter has been just a short guide to questioning. I hope that what comes through loud and clear here is that I use questioning very sparingly. But this is not about me; it's about you, and it's about your practice. Examine the questions that you ask within your therapy, and how your clients respond. To do this, I highly recommend recording your sessions (with the client's permission), listening back, and seeing what effect questions are having. Are they working for you? When they do work, why? If they didn't work, why not? Use what you find to refine to what extent – and how – you ask questions.

Chapter 8

The Skill of Challenge

THE SKILL OF CHALLENGE is also sometimes known as the skill of confrontation. To me, the words 'challenge' and 'confrontation' don't fit with my understanding of counselling. If I look to the dictionary definition of the verb 'to challenge', I see words like 'disagree', 'dispute' and 'take issue with'. The last thing I want to be doing in a counselling session is confronting the client. If I'm supposed to be with them empathically, within their frame of reference, standing next to them no matter how scary things get, confrontation just doesn't fit.

The words also bring stuff up for me as a person. In fact, I don't like confrontation. I feel a little panicky when I hear the word. It's very common to hear people say, 'I avoid confrontation.' Yet we have this advanced skill that we should be using in counselling.

Purpose of Confrontation

Of course, 'confront' can also mean 'face up to and deal with'. So maybe it's about the client facing up to and dealing with whatever it is that's going on for them. So why might we, as counsellors, use challenge within the therapeutic relationship?

Sometimes, a client – in bringing their material – might show an incongruence or mismatch between their thoughts and their feelings. We can't see this because it happens internally, but very often the client will give us a clue by saying something like, 'I shouldn't really be feeling like this.' Within the emotional world of this client, they're feeling a heaviness or pain, but within their head (cognitively), there's a thought that's saying, 'I shouldn't be feeling this way.'

Where else might we see a mismatch? It might be between the client's words and body language. For example, they might say, 'I'm OK. I can cope with this. I have no choice,' yet the tears are streaming down their face, their head falls into their hands and they sob as they speak. So despite those words of apparent coping, the body language is very clearly showing extreme pain and emotional distress; there is a definite incongruence.

Definition of Challenge in Counselling

Definitions can be dry, but are useful and necessary when writing assignments. Such a definition of challenge/confrontation might be: 'When the counsellor highlights an incongruence between the client's verbal and nonverbal communication so as to facilitate the client's awareness of conflicts relating to particular issues/topics'. In other words, it's about highlighting what the client is bringing and showing the incongruence/mismatch, so that the client can see that for themselves and choose to move from rigidity to fluidity, experiencing a moment of movement and questioning what is going on for them.

Challenging Gently

How might we be able to challenge the client in a gentle way, and from their own frame of reference? If we look back at the example of a client saying, 'I shouldn't be feeling this way,' we could respond, 'I hear you saying that you shouldn't be feeling this. I hear those words coming out of your mouth, but at the same time I recognise that what you're carrying at the moment is really heavy.'

There's a very gentle challenge: all we're doing is highlighting the incongruence of what the client is bringing to us within that moment. It's not from our frame of reference as the counsellor – we are fully integrated in the client's world. It doesn't feel challenging, but nevertheless it is. It's an invitation to the client to have a look and say, 'Yes, I'm saying it's OK but, my goodness, I'm feeling terrible.' We may see a moment of movement there, where they drop that thought of 'I shouldn't be thinking this' and they say, 'Yes, it is terrible,' fully submerged within that feeling. That incongruence can disintegrate in front of us.

We could also challenge the client who says, 'I'm OK. I can cope with this. I have no choice,' as the tears stream down their face. In that situation, we might say, 'I hear you saying that you're coping with this because you have to, yet at the same time I can't help but notice the tears that are streaming down your face, and it feels like you're totally broken within this.' The client has been acknowledged for that emotion that they're feeling, but the words that they've said are highlighted – that incongruence is once again brought out into the open. Again, it's an invitation to explore that mismatch.

> **"**
>
> **It's about highlighting what the client is bringing and showing the incongruence/ mismatch, so that the client can see that for themselves and choose to move from rigidity to fluidity, experiencing a moment of movement and questioning what is going on for them.**
>
> **"**

Using Challenge Safely

Challenge is an advanced skill. So don't go into a first session with a client, pull out the skill of challenge and pop it right there on the table! Doing this could bring about defensiveness. It could feel like criticism to the client, and mean they feel negative, put down and judged. I believe that if we are going to bring challenge into a session, there needs to be an established rapport. There needs to be a high level of support, so that the client perceives our unconditional positive regard (UPR) and knows that they are in a safe place when we use challenge.

Sometimes, a client may view us as the expert, with all the answers. If we challenge before we've built up trust and addressed the balance of power within the counselling relationship, the client could feel like there's something wrong with them. They could leave saying, 'Oh, there's something really wrong with me because the expert has pointed this out to me.' So we've got to be really careful when we're using challenge.

Recognising Good Challenge

What does challenge look like when it is used properly? As noted above, good challenge is really gentle and supportive; most importantly, it accurately reflects only what the client has shared. In other words, we put aside the thoughts and feelings that may arise within us ourselves and we bring only what the client has shared with us.

In her book *Skills in Person-Centred Counselling & Psychotherapy* (2016) – a book I love and would thoroughly recommend – Janet Tolan asserts that by the counsellor demonstrating the core conditions of empathy, congruence and UPR, challenge naturally arises within the client's self-concept.

For example, the client may believe that crying is a sign of weakness. So they tend to block their pain, swallowing their emotion – they don't want to show this to the world because they don't want to be perceived as weak. Of course, this is a faulty belief, but it feels true for the client. When the client brings their pain into the counselling room, the counsellor is fully there with them in that emotion (empathic understanding) and completely accepts it and them (UPR). This naturally challenges the client's idea that crying is weak.

Next Steps in Challenge

In closing, I want to acknowledge that challenge in counselling is not confrontational and negative: used sensitively, it can be so supportive and positive. For example, at the end of a series of counselling sessions, a client might say, 'Wow, I feel real movement and I'm now in a very different place.' We might reply: 'You know, when you came in, I noticed that you were like [that]. But now, you sit in front of me and you tell me you are like [this].' That is a challenge; it's a challenge to the client to look at the progress that they have made within the therapy.

I challenge you to speak to your peers about challenge. I challenge you to look for challenge within your own life. I challenge you to record your skill sessions and look whether you're using challenge. It is a powerful skill – an advanced skill, but a necessary one. Challenge exists in counselling.

Chapter 9
Idiosyncratic Empathy

EMPATHY IS NOT A COUNSELLING SKILL as such; it is more a way of being. It is very important because it underpins the skills that we might bring to a session. Our counselling skills – reflection, paraphrasing, nonverbal communication etc. – are all worthless unless we have empathy running through them.

Carl Rogers, in developing the person-centred approach to counselling, recognised empathy as being necessary within the therapeutic relationship to bring about psychological contact. But it doesn't matter which approach or model of counselling you look to: empathy must be present even in the more psychodynamic, psychoanalytical forms of therapy. Today, there is an increasing recognition that empathy and the therapeutic relationship are vital to effective therapy.

What is Empathy?

Empathy is about us, as counsellors, seeing the client's world as they see it – that is, from their frame of reference. And the empathy circle is complete only when we are able to communicate that back in such a way that the client understands we've seen it that way. It's when the client thinks, 'Yes, this person gets me,' that an empathic connection has been formed. This bond takes your relationship with that client to a deeper level: they are being heard; you understand them.

We're basically speaking about perception. We need to perceive what it is that the client is bringing, and to communicate that back in a way that makes the client feel they've been understood. So perception without communication is useless and is not empathy. For example, you might be reading a book or watching a movie that is emotional, and you become very involved in a character and feel a really strong bond with them. You are able to perceive that, but you are not able to communicate back to the actor or the person in the book. So the empathy cycle is not complete within that transaction.

But What about the 'Idiosyncratic'?

'Idiosyncratic' is defined as relating to the individual. So idiosyncratic empathy means that the empathy will be different depending on the person you are working with. If you are in the client's frame of reference, if you're really seeing things how they do, then empathy is going to be individual for each and every client. The term 'idiosyncratic empathy' was first coined by Jerold Bozarth. He recognised that empathy needed to be different depending on what the client was bringing, who they were, and what their frame of reference was.

Thus, with one client, you may find yourself laughing, with the tears rolling down your cheeks; that's fine if that's where the client is and what they are bringing on that day – you are with that client as they were full of joy, laughter and fun. With the next client, you may find yourself in a very different place.

Recognising Our Self-Concept

Empathy is not about you, as the counsellor, getting it right or wrong. It's about trying to be in the client's frame of reference and trying to get it right: almost melting yourself into that client's world and being there with them. In order to do this, we need to look at our own self-concept and know who we are as individuals, recognising that we bring our self-concept into the counselling relationship.

So what is our self-concept? It's the truths that we hold in life. It's everything that we believe. It's rooted in our culture, childhood, belief structure, race and sexuality. All these things form the way that we look at the world. We project this self-structure out onto everything that we look at.

The Importance of Personal Development

It is for this reason that counselling training is personal development (PD); it requires looking within. You may be familiar with the Johari window exercise. Certain things are unseen by us, but they may be visible to others. And part of the counselling journey, specifically in PD groups, is about encouraging those elements of our personality that are invisible to us – perhaps not-for-growth elements of ourselves – to come into our awareness, challenging us to look at them. It's about us examining our self-concept and what we believe is true – and readjusting that so we can be there fully with the client, looking at their material not through our own eyes but trying to do so through theirs.

The Importance of Not 'Rescuing'

For example, suppose a client says, 'I'm devastated. I'm so disgusted with myself. I'm so terribly overweight. When I look in the mirror, I just see this ugly, fat person.' That's tough material. That's a hurt person who's in a really difficult place. Hearing that, how would you respond in an empathic way, being in that client's frame of reference?

You may be tempted to say, 'Well, I hear what you're saying but that's not what I see. I see a beautiful individual in front of me.' That would be 100% in my own frame of reference. I'm basically saying to that client, 'No, you're wrong. What you're perceiving and what you're seeing is not right. Let me tell you what I see here.' And that is really not empathic. That is not being in the client's frame of reference and that client will certainly not feel heard. They may feel rescued – like I've thrown them a life-jacket – but they're not going to feel heard or validated.

> "
>
> **We're not trying to rescue them from the pain of what they feel towards their own self; we're understanding it. That's what empathy is all about**
>
> "

Using Idiosyncratic Empathy

So idiosyncratic empathy is about reflecting back in a way that allows the client to feel heard. So maybe the empathic response in the situation described above might be something along the lines of, 'Wow, that sounds so terribly destroying for you that when you look in the mirror, you just see this fat person that you basically can't stand, and recognise that it is you.' That's certainly not rescuing the client. It's empathic and in their frame of reference. We're not trying to rescue them from the pain of what they feel towards their own self; we're understanding it. That's what empathy is all about.

Using Questions in Counselling

As soon as we find ourselves asking questions for any reason other than to clarify our full understanding of that client's frame of reference, we're in our own frame of reference and we break empathy. We're now saying to the client, 'Hey, well, what happens if you do this, and what about that, and what about the next thing? Yeah, but have you tried this?' That is not within the client's frame of reference and it is certainly not empathic.

If we are operating as person-centred counsellors, we avoid asking any questions other than to clarify our understanding. The cycle is complete with what the client brings, how we perceive that, and how we understand that. It's not about us being right, but rather about:

- being fully integrated within the client's frame of reference
- putting aside our own self-concept
- being truly with the client just for that moment
- reflecting back our understanding in such a way that the client thinks, 'Yes, you hear me.'

Developing Our Feelings Vocabulary

Part of being empathic is having a vocabulary to be able to describe what we perceive a client to be bringing. So if we're empathically connected to a client, how can we put that in words to feed back to them?

It's interesting that there are so many different ways to say things. For example, it's said that there are many Inuit words for snow. But human beings often have very few words for their emotions. We can say 'happy', 'sad' or 'angry'. But these seem very basic words for the underlying emotions.

Part of being reflective is looking within ourselves at our own emotions, and pinpointing words to describe them. This is best done by processing your day and maybe journaling. As you do this, think what word really fits with this – because if we can find words to describe our emotions and feelings, maybe we can use those words within a counselling relationship to reflect back our understanding of what a client is bringing. We may find that when we use a certain word, this really resonates for the client, and they go, 'Wow, yeah. Wow, that's the word. That's exactly it.'

Fine-tuning Our Feelings Words

For instance, a client might say, 'They laid me off from my job.' You notice that their fists and teeth are clenched as they speak to you. And you see the muscles in their neck tensing up. Would 'angry' be right word for that? Or might 'furious' more accurately capture the strength of their feeling? It's about having a vocabulary that kind of turns the dial from mildly irritated right through to absolutely fuming.

As you're saying the word that you feel to the client, how do you intonate it? Do you sit there calmly and say, 'You know, you look absolutely furious'? Or do you mirror their body language and say, 'Wow, you're furious!' The latter helps to put the feeling of what you're perceiving from the client into the words that you feed back to them. This is idiosyncratic empathy; it's empathy in motion. It's happening right there and then within those moments. It really is vital to develop your vocabulary, so you can interpret what the client is bringing and add words to unnamed feelings.

Next Steps in Using Idiosyncratic Empathy

- Take idiosyncratic empathy into your next simulated skills session and see how it is ever-changing and liquid – as individual as the clients that you will have the privilege of being with on their journey. If you work first with one of your peers and then with another, how different is that empathy within those two relationships?

- If you're merely reflecting back the words the client gave, is that really an empathic connection? Are you looking to the individual person? Are you recognising their body language – for example, where are they looking and what are they doing with their hands? What type of tone are they using when they speak? We must look way beyond the words, to the person that is there bringing those words.

- Have a chat with your peers about what empathy means to them. Explain what it means to you. Get their differing opinions.

Chapter 10

The Skill of Simile
and Metaphor

FIRST, IT IS IMPORTANT TO DEFINE what simile and metaphor are – there is often confusion among learners of what the difference is between these two types of imagery. To put it in plain English, similes tend to hit you over the head with a comparison. They often use the words 'like' or 'as'. So, to use the example of some lyrics from a Bon Jovi song, 'My heart is like an open highway,' that's a simile.

Meanwhile, a metaphor is a word or a phrase that also makes a comparison (e.g. between people, places or things), but it requires a cultural understanding – and says that the person, for example, actually is (rather than is like) something. So, for instance, if I said to you, 'Rory is a walking encyclopaedia when it comes to counselling theory,' you would understand that I mean he knows a lot (rather than wondering whether I realised that books don't really have legs!).

When Clients Use Imagery

You will come across simile and metaphor within your counselling relationships. For instance, you might have a client who comes in and says, 'I have a knot in my stomach.' Of course, the truth is they don't literally have a knot in their stomach; they are using a metaphor to describe a feeling they're experiencing. Or they might say, 'I feel like a caged animal' (using a simile).

So why do clients use metaphors and similes? Basically, it's a shortcut in language. It creates an understanding between two people. But also, it is sometimes easier for the client to speak in images – in pictures, in an abstract way – than it is for them to speak about the real pain that they're bringing. The truth is that when somebody comes into therapy, the chances are that they will have spent very little time actually naming their feelings before.

Developing Our Feelings Vocabulary

As counsellors and psychotherapists, we are encouraged – as part of our journey – to keep a process journal. This is fantastic, in that we get to look at what we feel within the day, and to start putting names to those feelings that we have within us, so we get to understand them. It becomes a language that we are comfortable with. But when a client comes in, it's almost like they have illiteracy in this area. How often in everyday conversation do people find themselves talking about feelings? It is rare. They may express very simple feelings – say, 'I feel quite happy' or 'I'm feeling a bit down' – but, as counsellors, we're expected to have a better grasp of (and so a wider vocabulary for) feelings.

To help develop this, you could develop a feelings list that outlines some different words you can use. So if we're talking, say, about fear, we could use 'apprehension', 'dread', 'foreboding', 'fright', 'mistrust' or 'panic'. There are many words that we can use to tag onto common feelings. Clients may not have easy access to these words, so they default to what they know.

There's no doubt it's easier to speak in pictures. Children speak in metaphor and simile all the time, and they understand if we do the same. So it's very common that a client will come in and say, 'I'm wound up like a coiled spring,' meaning that they're really tense.

Using Imagery as a Counsellor

Of course, it's not just the client who can bring simile and metaphor into the therapeutic relationship. We, as counsellors, can do that as well. We can reflect back in metaphor and simile what we're seeing. Imagery is all about empathic connection: it's about two people in a situation having a shared understanding.

For example, the counsellor might say, 'Wow, it feels like you might be drowning in your life.' Of course, the client isn't literally drowning, but that metaphor paints the picture that they're unable to keep their head above water, that they feel that they're being pulled down. There may be a sense of huge panic that goes with that. If that image resonates with the client, they might respond, 'And I don't have a life vest.' And we might reply, 'There's nobody there for you. You feel that the waters are coming over you and there's just nothing to keep you up.'

So it's perfectly acceptable for you to bring in metaphor and simile – so long as you have established a deep empathic bond with your client, and you feel it is appropriate.

Communicating on the Edge of Awareness

Imagery can allow or empower the client to communicate how they feel about things that are still on the edge of their awareness. American psychotherapist Eugene Gendlin spoke of this as being a felt sense – where the client can't quite put words to it, so they use descriptive images to bring that to you.

Communicating About 'the Dark Times'

Clients may also find it easier to talk in terms of imagery than about what really happened. For example, a client may refer to 'the dark times' rather than 'the times when I was being abused'. This is where we – as counsellors or psychotherapists – can continue this imagery, using it as a vehicle and as something that is external to the client.

In her book *Skills in Person Centred Counselling & Psychotherapy*, Janet Tolan uses a descriptive example of a trapped animal. The client might say, 'I feel like a caged animal.' And the counsellor might reflect back and say, 'You're trapped. There's just no way out of where you are at the moment. You're frightened. You're panicky.' And then the client may come back and say, 'And I'm helpless. I've got no teeth. I've got no claws.' As the counsellor, we might speak to the metaphor and respond, 'What is it that animal needs right now?'

> "
> **Imagery is all about empathic connection: it's about two people in a situation having a shared understanding.**
> "

In this way, we would be speaking in the third person to our client in the room. We're speaking to the picture that they have brought because there's safety in that image for them. The client can relate to this because it is part of self; the safety allows a re-framing, where they can stand externally to the situation and see what it is that this frightened, trapped animal really needs. Maybe the client says, 'Just to be loved, to be recognised.' Of course, it's clear that these needs relate to the client, and we can even reflect that back, saying, 'You just need to be loved, to be recognised.'

Being Cautious with Imagery

Working with simile and metaphor takes place at great relational depth (Mearns and Cooper, 2005), but we do need to tread carefully. There are dangers in using metaphor because it is culture-specific. It is a shared understanding, but a cultural shared understanding. So it would be highly inappropriate to refer with a Jewish client to 'bringing home the bacon,' because that metaphor just wouldn't sit well with them culturally.

So we do need to watch and be really careful that we are in the client's frame of reference. For instance, if a client said, 'It's like being a Liverpool supporter on match day,' does this mean they are feeling elation or misery? It's about trying to find out where they're coming from, to understand their cultural reference point. Doing so is vital to creating an empathic bond, and so to using the power of imagery within the counselling relationship.

Next Steps in Using Imagery in Counselling

- Think about imagery – process it, write about it, and journal about where you use metaphor and simile in your everyday life, and what certain things mean culturally to you.

- Listen out for the imagery you hear used by your friends, in the media, and in literature and films.

- Discuss metaphor and simile with your peers on your counselling training course.

- When you're next in a simulated skills session, watch out for similes and metaphors. Do you see a picture being brought in? If you go with that picture and really drill deep down into it, how far does that go?

I know I've had clients who have brought a picture into their counselling sessions – maybe two or three sessions in – and they're still using that same image after 10 or 11 sessions. It has become a common theme that weaves itself through their work. In short, simile and metaphor can be really powerful in the counselling room.

Chapter 11
The Skill of Immediacy

IMMEDIACY IS AN ADVANCED COUNSELLING SKILL. You would look to use it only once the therapeutic relationship had been formed, and so once there was great trust between counsellor and client. The pay-off – if immediacy does hit home with the client – is immense: they will have a strong feeling that they have been heard and understood.

However, immediacy is risky. If you get it wrong (which is bound to happen sometimes), it kind of fractures the relationship for a few moments. It's like the client is feeling, 'No, you really don't get me here; that is totally off.' When this happens, you need to be able to fall back on your shared trust and the relational depth (Mearns and Cooper, 2005) in order to be able to move past this. Immediacy is therefore not something that you would try in the first session or even at the very beginning of a session with an established client.

What is Immediacy?

The person-centred approach to counselling suggests that generally we should be 100% in the client's frame of reference – that we don't bring our frame of reference into the counselling session at all. Immediacy is the one exception to this. It expresses something that comes up in you as the counsellor; it's a gut feeling. We all know that instinctive feeling we sometimes get that just can't be explained or measured. We're talking something metaphysical: some might call it a hunch. In counselling, this is referred to as 'immediacy'.

Basically, using immediacy means you are going to be revealing how you, as the counsellor, are thinking, feeling or sensing; of those three verbs, the strongest for me is 'sensing'. It's very human, because you're sharing a little bit of yourself, of what you see, and of how this looks to you.

An Example of Immediacy

For example, say you're working with a client who is bringing his material. As he does so, you look at him. All of a sudden, the client appears to you as a lost little boy. Immediacy is being right there in the here-and-now, immediately sharing your sense with the client. You might say: 'As you say that, I sense that you look like a lost little boy.' Now that's not within the client's frame of reference; it's not even on the client's edge of awareness. Rather, it is 100% within your own frame of reference as the counsellor – but it's a feeling that is strong and very present within the counselling relationship, so you share it.

When your words hit home, two things could happen:

- The client might take that and reply: 'You know what? That's exactly how it feels. I feel like I'm seven years old again – unbelievable.' Then there might be a silence, while the client really goes there. This would mean that the immediacy had hit home; the resonance is magnificent.

> "
> **There might be a silence, while the client really goes there. This would mean that the immediacy had hit home; the resonance is magnificent**
> "

- The client looks at you quizzically, like he has been completely pulled out of where he was at. You've got it wrong; that's OK. What I would do in that situation is be congruent and say: 'It looks like I got that wrong, and you're not there at all?' This would invite the client to share where he is at and to put you firmly and squarely back into his frame of reference.

Should I Go for It?

In summary, to use immediacy safely, you need trust within the relationship, and you need boundaries to be well-established. You are sharing a part of yourself with the client. When this resonates and hits home, it is highly effective and really does take the counselling relationship to a completely new level. It is, I guess, linked in a way to idiosyncratic empathy, in that it is unique both to the particular situation and to the individual client.

When you feel a strong sense building up within you during a counselling session, you might come up against an internal filter that says: 'Should I – or shouldn't I – say this?' As soon as you start wondering this, you're no longer 100% there in the moment. So what I would suggest is to dive in: take the plunge and try it! Share that gut feeling you have with the client you've been working with for some time, where the relationship is deep and trusting, and see what happens.

Can I Try Immediacy in Skills Practice?

Immediacy is a magical and very powerful skill; like all the other counselling skills, it takes time to develop. It is difficult to use immediacy in simulated skill sessions – that is, when you are sitting in a classroom. This is because you don't really have the opportunity to get to the relational depth at which immediacy would be appropriate, since you may be working with different colleagues from week to week. This is in contrast to when you're working with a client: you're seeing them on a regular basis and that relationship is continually deepening and developing.

In short, do try immediacy within your client sessions, when the time feels right. Trust yourself and see its effect on your counselling relationships.

Chapter 12

The Seven Stages of Process

CARL ROGERS DEVELOPED THE THEORY of the seven stages of process, perhaps best explained in his book *On Becoming a Person*, originally published in 1961. This chapter aims leaves skills for a moment to relate this theory to practice, bringing it into the therapy room and our relationship with the client. How can the theory inform practice and thus what skills we should use? What we can look out for? How we can see these stages in motion?

This chapter is based on text taken from Merry, T. & Lusty, B. (1993) *What is Person – Centred Therapy?*, Loughton, Essex: Gale Centre Publications.

http://www.inter-psyche.co.uk/upload/Rogers_7_stages_of_counselling.pdf

From Fixity to Fluidity

In his book, Rogers wrote (1961, p. 100): 'Individuals move, I began to see, not from fixity or homeostasis through change to a new fixity, though such a process is indeed possible. But much the more significant continuum is from fixity to changingness, from rigid structure to flow, from stasis to process.' That's a great quote to use in an assignment, but what exactly does it mean?

What Rogers is saying is not that a person comes in with one set of rigid and fixed views and goes through a process within the therapeutic relationship whereby those views change to different fixed views. Rather, it's a process of going from having really fixed and rigid ways of looking at the world to being a more fully functioning person through a loosening of self-structure. So it is about being more open, fluid and accepting.

Seven Non-Linear Stages

According to Rogers, this process can be split into seven stages. At stage one, the organism is fixed, rigid, stuck, anxious and incongruent – while at stage seven, it is fluid, spontaneous and congruent. When Rogers speaks about the 'organism', he is referring to us and our clients as humans – to the way we are and to the way we interact with our world. In this chapter, we look at Rogers' seven stages, examining how they fit into our counselling relationships.

The seven stages are not a linear process: clients can move backwards and forwards between stages at any time, though this is much less likely at the later stages.

Stage One

Rogers (1961, p. 132) describes the first stage as follows: 'The individual in this stage of fixity and remoteness of experience is not likely to come voluntarily for therapy.' In other words, it is unlikely as therapists that we're going to be seeing a person who is in stage one – an extremely rigid, fixed position in terms of their views of the world.

Rogers identifies that there is an unwillingness to communicate any part of self: communication is always about external factors. So a person at stage one will see any kind of pain that they experience within their life as being due to purely external influences, i.e. outside their control. They will say that people, places and things cause them difficulty: 'Oh, that's a terrible place. You don't want to be going there' or 'Those kind of people are [such and such].' They feel that talking about their feelings is a waste of time.

Although it's highly unlikely that a person at stage one will walk into our therapy room, it is not impossible. For example, a client might arrive and – when we ask them why they have come to therapy – say, for example, "My wife said I should come' or (in school/college counselling), 'My teacher said I need to come and see you.' This is something that's really worth looking out for, because if a client comes in and implies they're not there for themselves, how can we build a therapeutic relationship with them? Is it even ethical for us to engage in therapy if a person feels that they are only there because somebody else suggested that they come in?

Rogers identifies that the person in stage one will not be able to notice and recognise the feelings within self – so there will be nothing to process. There is a complete incongruence in this client entering therapy. And it may well be that the ethical thing to do, if the client says that someone else suggested they should come, is to say, 'Well, what do you feel about that?' They might then reply: 'Well, I don't think I've got any problems. If anyone's got a problem here, it's the teacher', so externalising all of the responsibility. An ethical response might be: 'Well, you know that I'm here if you need me, and if you ever feel that you want to engage, you can always come back into therapy.' This allows them to leave, because there is no therapeutic process going to take place with this person.

Stage Two

So what might we see at stage two? How might we recognise a stage-two person in our therapy room? First, we're going to see a slight loosening of the rigid constructs, although we're still going to notice that the client may present themselves with having difficulty in accepting any kind of responsibility for their feelings. So they may appear as a victim within their own life: everything that is happening to them will once again be externalised. We may find them saying that they're living in a hostile world: 'If you had a [job/wife/children] like mine, you too would feel this way.'

How they look at the world is for them a fact, because the concept of self is still very rigid. Because of this, they don't see that they have the ability to influence their happiness within the world. It's almost like the world imposes its will upon them. But what we may see is that they start to acknowledge that feelings are there, even if they don't recognise them as such. These emotions will be just underneath the surface – on the edge of awareness.

We may be able to start working with a client who is in stage two. They may again use very broad statements, for example, 'It's always like that, isn't it?' The 'isn't it?' is a great indicator of a stage-two client, because they're starting to question where they're coming from. They're feeling this pain and recognising – at least to a minimal degree – that there is some kind of feeling within them, although they may not be able to verbalise or pinpoint that. But it is there: it's on that edge of awareness. They might start to show tendencies to question and explore what they are feeling.

People at stage two may define themselves and where they are in the here-and-now in terms of their past lives. So we may hear statements like, 'I can never get [such and such] right', 'I'm always finding myself in this situation' or 'I could never do something like that.' It's almost like they are evidencing where they are in the here-and-now in terms of past negative experiences. These are the kinds of clues that we might get if we're seeing a client in stage two.

What can we do as therapists if we recognise that a client is at stage two? First, we can make sure we are right there in that client's frame of reference with our empathic understanding of what it is like for them. It's not our job as counsellors to move them from stage two to stage three. It is only our job to provide those necessary and sufficient conditions that Rogers identified as being the building blocks that allow, encourage and empower the client to move by themselves. We can reflect back exactly how we perceive their world for them, trust in the process, and allow the client to find their own way.

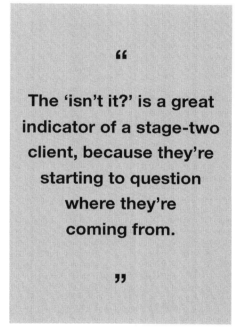

"

The 'isn't it?' is a great indicator of a stage-two client, because they're starting to question where they're coming from.

"

Stage Three

At stage three, there's a slight loosening of that rigidity of attitudes seen at stages one and two. We might find that this client is more willing to talk about themselves, so there is the acknowledgement that they feel pain, and that this pain is theirs. However, they may seem more comfortable talking about the pain of the past than about the here-and-now pain they are experiencing in current daily life. An example of that might be: 'When I was a kid, I did a lot of things that made me feel really bad.'

In a client at stage three, we may see the incongruence starting to show. We begin to see contradictions in what they think and feel coming out within the counselling relationship. For example, they might say: 'I try so hard to be the perfect partner, but I fail all time. It always goes wrong.' We're seeing the intention, but the feeling inside is contradicting that: we're seeing that incongruence manifesting itself in the words the client is bringing.

Also at stage three, we're going to notice that the client is open to different possibilities and points of view. In contrast to the stage-one and stage-two view that what they project out to the world is the only way, the stage-three client is more accepting of the idea that there are other ways of doing things – though still with a tendency to default to what their self-concept tells them.

So how might we work with a client who we recognise to be at stage three? We need to use unconditional positive regard (UPR), accepting them just as they are. They will then begin to unravel the stories themselves and to delve in deeply, as we reflect and use our skills to put that back in front of them. That UPR allows them to feel safe, to be open and to look at different ideas, concepts and ways of seeing the world. They will be bringing parts of self that they may find unacceptable: 'Oh, I shouldn't be this way.' As counsellors, we can accept that as part of them, unconditionally and without judgement. In seeing our acceptance, the stage-three client – being open to other inputs and ways of looking at things – may themselves start to accept that and move towards stage four.

Stage Four

So what are we likely to see at stage four in a client's presentation? First, we're going to notice that there is once again a loosening of that self-construct. The client is beginning to describe more intense feelings, but is still much more comfortable bringing past rather than here-and-now feelings, for example: 'I felt so desperately unhappy when she didn't seem to care. I've never known such deep feelings. It really scared me.' Notice how all those verbs are in the past tense: 'felt', 'known' and 'scared' rather than 'feel', 'know' and 'scares'. Rogers uses the beautiful phrase 'the not now' to describe this phenomenon. It's entirely understandable: those feelings are painful and they're hurtful, so why would the client want to experience them in the here-and-now? It's like a form of protection.

The stage-four client really has difficulty understanding and accepting these negative feelings within self. They're more likely to want to run away from them, and putting them into the past is one way of doing that. It's avoiding the pain at all costs as opposed to embracing it and recognising it as part of self. It's almost for this client as if they would rather that the pain had never existed in the first place.

However at stage four, we're going to notice that the client may accidentally bring here-and-now feelings into the therapy session. When this does happen, they will generally mistrust or reject those emotions. For example, the client may say, 'There's this deep knot here, right down deep inside and it stops me from being myself. I don't know what it is, and it makes me angry. What can I do about it?' So the feeling is there, in the here-and-now, but it's not accepted, embraced or even fully seen as part of self. The client is trying to distance themselves from it, running away from it and looking for the switch to turn it off.

While at stages one to three, there was an externalisation of why the client was feeling the pain (as if the responsibility for that pain rested with other people, places and things), the stage-four client starts to own what is happening. However, the fearfulness of doing so, and the hopelessness of the situation, are going to be very apparent. For example, the client may say something: 'I'm feeling terrible, and I don't know what it is. It must just be me; there must be something wrong with me.' There's a clear acceptance of responsibility, but total helplessness surrounding that.

We may find at stage four that the client has difficulty trusting the therapist, and this again is understandable. They've had difficulty trusting – and so want to distance themselves from – their own feelings. They're having difficulty trusting that they themselves form a part of their world and are in some way responsible for how their life has turned out, and so for the way they feel. So for them to put trust unquestioningly in the therapist is really difficult. You may hear the client verbalising that: 'I find it really difficult to trust people', 'I don't know if this is going to work for me', 'How do I know if this is the right modality for me?' or 'How do I know that you are the right counsellor?'

> **While at stages one to three, there was an externalisation of why the client was feeling the pain ... the stage-four client starts to own what is happening.**

Finally, we can sometimes see an inappropriate use of humour by the client, who may bring pain but then laugh. Or they might describe something really painful and then say: 'You probably just think I'm mad.' Another clue here can be talking about self using the third person: 'It's crazy, isn't it? I can't believe a man in his 40s would keep on getting into these situations. Look at me!' It's like they are distancing themselves from the responsibility, and using humour to deflect fully accepting and embracing the feeling.

So how do we work with this client? Very often, we're going to be working with clients at stage four. The main thing is just to be with them, providing UPR and empathy, being congruent and using our counselling skills. That's all we need to do. We're there to provide a threat-free environment where the client can begin to trust more, can begin to bring more of self, and can maybe move onto the fifth of the seven stages of process.

Stage Five

At stage five, we're starting to see that the client is more confident about what they're feeling in the here-and-now, they're happier to express presently experienced feelings, and they recognise these as their own emotions. There's a deepening of the trust – and so of the level at which we work: the relational depth (Mearns and Cooper, 2005). As the client brings these here-and-now feelings, the emotions are less denied to self and more accepted. While the client tended to distance themselves from difficult feelings at stage four, they now might say: 'OK, this feeling is here and it's mine, and I'm fine to look at it right now.'

> **It's at the fifth stage that we see those light-bulb moments in which the client has new insights into their life and relationships.**

They can start to have feelings 'bubbling up' (as Rogers puts it) inside them. And while the client may not fully understand or accept these, they do find ways of expressing them within the therapy relationship. For example, the stage-five client might say: 'I've just realised that when I start feeling unsure of myself, I get this strange feeling. It feels like a weight pushing down on my chest, and it fills me up with all this anxiety. As I'm speaking about it, I can actually feel it now.'

Of course, there's still a fear of the pain of embracing these feelings and being totally overwhelmed by them in the present. So we may find at stage five that a client gets close to something, kind of teeters on the edge, and then pulls back, not being able to fully submerge themselves in here-and-now feelings. We may also notice that there's a reluctance to fully trust the feelings that they're having. In this sense, a client may appear to be at stages four and five at the same time.

However, it's at the fifth stage that we see those light-bulb moments in which the client has new insights into their life and relationships. For example, a client might say: 'I've carried this massive resentment for my father because of what he did when I was a child. And I felt so bad about that, about what I've been holding inside. He's my father, I shouldn't feel that way, but now I look at it, I think it's OK for me to be angry about that. I should be angry. I guess I still love him. I still love him, but what he did was wrong, and I'm OK to be angry about that.' At stage five, the client is almost saying: 'It's OK for me to have these negative emotions. They are part of who I am.'

Stage Six

Rogers described the sixth stage of the seven stages of process as being very distinctive and often very dramatic. We're talking about life-changing events here. When clients have realisations that stick with them, they're not transient in the way they might have been at earlier stages. So it's unlikely that a client at stage six will regress.

At stage six, all feelings are fully experienced in the present moment – accurately, clearly and meaningfully. Instead of seeing these emotions as a negative experience – and so wanting to avoid them or mistrusting them – the client accepts them as part of self. This gives them the power to change who they are, to grow, and to see the world in a new way. Ambiguities, incongruence and uncertainty dissolve.

We may see the client starting to talk about their own self-care, looking at themselves with tenderness. They may say: 'When I look back and see myself at ten years old, with all the pain I was going through at that time, I want to give myself a hug.' The client fully embraces and loves themselves. As Rogers points out, it is a curious paradox that in order to be able to change, we must first truly accept ourselves as we are.

Stage Seven

I touch on stage seven only briefly, as it is unlikely that we will have a client in our therapy room at this stage. After the profound and irreversible experiences of stage six, there is going only to be growth, and it is unlikely the client will feel they need a counsellor to facilitate this. Instead, they will find that growth in their own life as they continue to fully accept themselves, and to examine the moment-to-moment feelings that they have in the here-and-now. So stage seven is very much about self-growth.

Conclusion

I find it fascinating to look at the seven stages of process, seeing the journey that a person might come on – from stage one, where we are unlikely to see a client engaging in therapy, right through to stage seven, where we are again unlikely to see a client engaging in therapy! It is truly a movement from fixity, through gradual loosening of the self-concept, to fluidity – in other words, to being a fully functioning person.

"

It is a curious paradox that in order to be able to change, we must first truly accept ourselves as we are.

"

Chapter 13
Endings in Counselling

THINK NOW ABOUT A TIME when you, in your own life, experienced a sudden and unexpected ending. It may have been the death of a loved one (human or animal), the loss of a job (e.g. where you went into work one day and were told you were no longer needed), or the end of a relationship. How does that ending feel for you? What kind of emotions are still with you from that unexpected ending? For example, there might be a feeling of helplessness. It's amazing how long the emotions relating to ending can be with us after the actual ending itself.

Now try to recall a time when you felt something was dragging on and on, and you just wished that it would end. It might be a relationship that you were unhappy in, yet you somehow felt unable to say: 'This isn't working for me.' So you stayed there, just hoping something would change. Or it could be a job that you hated for years but felt trapped in. Or how about those visitors who just won't leave? They don't take the hint when you say, 'Well, look at the time,' and, 'Oh, we have to be up early in the morning.' Instead, they just laugh and carry on! How does that memory feel for you? Let's try to relate these emotions to our counselling practice, and to our clients.

Endings are Tricky

Endings can be tricky. You need only look at complaints received by the British Association for Counselling and Psychotherapy – many relate to endings. For example, a client might feel that they were abandoned, or that the therapy stretched on longer than they needed it to.

The endings that we're going to be approaching with our clients are going to take place right there in the therapy room. Either we or the client is going to raise the possibility of ending. Human beings can sometimes feel resistant to endings: why might that be? Perhaps it's because an ending somehow implies that there's going to be a change – that the client is no longer going to be coming to seeing you and having that support. Also, of course, we tend to be naturally resistant to change. As human beings, we have a tendency to seek to avoid loss. It's interesting – when you look to psychological studies – to find that we are more motivated by the fear of loss than we are by the promise of gain. It's a massive factor and it's hardwired into the human condition.

Dangers of Avoiding Endings

One danger of ignoring the need to end within a therapeutic relationship is that we can create a situation where the client becomes dependent on coming to us for counselling. We might spot signs of this in clients – for example, if they say, 'I wouldn't be able to manage in life if it wasn't for you.' Rather than the counselling process being an empowering journey for the client, helping them to be self-sufficient, it then becomes disempowering: the client is projecting their power onto you, seeing you as their lifeline, anchor and support.

> "
> It's interesting ... to find that we are more motivated by the fear of loss than we are by the promise of gain.
> "

You may be in a session and feel that the therapeutic work is done – that what the client wanted to get out of counselling when they first came into your room, they have now got. You can clearly feel that their goal has been met, yet they continue to come back. It can be difficult, as the counsellor, to know how to raise the topic of ending. If we do dare do so, the client can seem surprised and almost taken aback by the fact that we should mention ending.

Ending is a Process

An ending is more of a process, not a sudden halt. It's not just something that suddenly happens one day. As Irvin Yalom (1975, p. 365) puts it in his book *The Theory and Practice of Group Psychotherapy*, 'Termination is more than an act signifying the end of therapy. It's an integral part of the process of therapy and, if properly understood and managed, may be an important factor in the instigation of change.'

The process of ending involves acknowledging the apparent readiness for this when we first see it and feel it to be appropriate – or it may be that the client acknowledges it and brings it into the relationship first. This may feel scary, because of our resistance to change. For some clients, endings are seen as traumatic for their self-concept, perhaps due to having experienced difficult separation early in life. This experience can cause great anxiety that can later affect the way that we act and interact with other people.

Stages of Planned Endings

I suggest here that there are three stages of a planned ending, but it is important not to take this as a blueprint for all clients. How you end will depend very much on the idiosyncratic relationship that you share with each client. Ending must fit with client needs, meaning that one size certainly doesn't fit all.

Stage 1: Assessing Readiness to End

First, we must assess the client's readiness to end. It might seem that they have reached their initial goals for therapy – but on the other hand, perhaps new and heavy material has surfaced that we feel needs dealing with.

If we do think a client may be ready to end, how can we introduce that into the therapeutic relationship? Maybe the client might say, 'When I came in here, I was really struggling with such and such, and I really feel that it's a lot easier for me to cope with that now.' That is a great invitation. So we might reply, 'I hear what you're saying. When you came in here, you were looking to do [x, y and z], and now here you are telling me that you're finding that you're able to cope with doing [x, y and z] … I just can't help but feel that we may be approaching the end of our time together.'

The pause in there is to kind of suggest that idea to the client. It's not that we're ending the sessions there, saying that this is the last time we'll meet. Instead, we're suggesting that we are approaching the end of our time together, implying that there is an approach – a process – of moving towards that ending. It's important to allow the client time to reflect, and also to observe their body language as a clue to how they are feeling about the idea of ending.

If the client responds, 'Oh no, I don't want this to end. I really value what we have here,' you can then work with that, acknowledging that the client (assuming the number of sessions is not time-limited by the agency) does have the power to decide when ending feels right to them. That would be the person-centred ideal – giving that back to the client to make the decision. But you, as the counsellor, nonetheless have a responsibility to acknowledge that possible readiness to end when you see it. It's about congruence, and not about creating dependence within the counselling relationship.

It's possible that the client may be devastated by the idea of ending. This hasn't happened in my experience a lot, but it can happen, and you may misread the client's readiness to end because we are only human. So if you do introduce the idea and it does feel like a bomb going off within your counselling relationship, think about how you might repair the fracture, reconstructing the therapeutic relationship so that you can continue as you were with the client.

> **"**
>
> **You ... have a responsibility to acknowledge that possible readiness to end when you see it. It's about congruence, and not about creating dependence within the counselling relationship.**
>
> **"**

Of course, it's different when it's the client that brings up the idea of ending. If the client says, 'I think I've got everything I need out of this and I'm on my merry way now, thank you very much,' then it's their right to do that.

Other possible signs that the client may be ready to end include that the counselling relationship has become less therapeutic and more chatty, that the client arrives late and/or misses appointments, or that there is joking and intellectualising within the session. Of course, each of these may also have other meanings/causes, or be a one-off occurrence, but if a pattern seems to be emerging, it is worth exploring whether the client feels they no longer need counselling.

Stage 2: Acknowledging the Relationship

After assessing the client's readiness, we need to acknowledge the power of the therapeutic relationship – because the client is ending not only their therapy but also their relationship with you. Relationships are very special places to be and can be mutually beneficial. It may be that you too value this relationship.

During the sessions you have shared, a therapeutic relationship has built up. The client may have said things to you that they have never spoken about to another human being, because they felt so safe here. The relationship has been at such depth that ending it is like a break-up. We therefore have to acknowledge the ending of our relationship.

Stage 3: Empowering the Client

Once we have agreed that the time is right to prepare to end, the third stage in the planned ending is to empower the client, increasing their self-sufficiency and resilience. This links right into the self-belief of the client.

A good analogy might relate to water, and I have found this useful as an image to use when speaking to clients who are ending.

Sometimes, going into counselling is like being a leaf that is on really choppy water. The water is whooshing and swooshing, and it's turbulent and unpleasant: the client is tumbling around and just can't find themselves. Through the counselling, perhaps the client feels that the water has become calmer, so that they're now bobbing and floating along, going down that stream.

This doesn't mean that they're never going to face rapid water again – or that there won't be rocks around the corner, because that's the nature of life. And it's fine to acknowledge this with your client, and to say: 'If ever you do find yourself in that tumble of life again and you feel you want to reach out, you know exactly where I am, and I would welcome that call.' That feels appropriate for me, though I accept it is easier in private practice than in an agency, where you may have a set amount of sessions that you are able to give to the client.

I've found that this metaphor really resonates with some clients; it's a pictorial way of showing than ending doesn't mean 'never again' – more 'for now' – and it's an acknowledgement that life does go on after that ending.

Different Kinds of Endings

There are various kinds of endings that we might face in counselling. First, the client may be going on holiday or taking a break, and may be in a really vulnerable place. It is an ending of your sessions for a period of time. How could you work with the client to help them manage and feel safe during that time? Or you, as counsellor, may be going on holiday yourself: when do you introduce that information to your client, and how do you manage that within the therapeutic relationship?

The best practice here is to tell your client as soon as you know that you'll be away. And the longer that you have been seeing your client, the longer the lead time you should ideally give. For example, you might say: 'Just to let you know, I will be away in two months' time, from [date] to [date]. I'm not assuming that you will still be coming then, but I just feel it's respectful to let you know.' Nearer the time, you might say: 'I wonder how you might manage while I'm away and how you might feel during that time.' Invite them to respond, and work on that in therapy.

Second, we have the planned ending – this is the 'fairytale' kind of ending. In our learning environments as student counsellors, we tend to look in detail at this type of ending, including best practice.

But what about the third type of ending – unplanned? This happens when the client just doesn't come back. You have a relationship that you've formed, and you don't know why they haven't come back. How does that feel for you, as the counsellor? Of course, supervision can help here, as can processing our thoughts and feelings through writing in a journal.

Fourth, every individual session has an ending. Every single time you start a session with a client, it's going to have an ending. At the start, during contracting, you'll outline how much time you have, and as the end is approaching, you'll mention that there is, say, five minutes to go. This is a way of acknowledging the ending, of starting the process of ending that session. But what about the client who just continues, right up to the very end: what does that bring up for you and how do you manage that kind of an ending with your client?

Working with Limited Sessions

Last but not least, there is the ending that you have no control of – where a client has only a set number of sessions, because of agency policy. Of course, the client will be aware of this from your very first session, when you will explain this in the contract. But if you are on the next-to-last session and this client is still carrying really heavy material (e.g. historic abuse), what can do? You're now approaching an ending, but it doesn't feel like a respectful one for this client. Could you possibly negotiate more sessions? Or could you refer this client on to somebody else who may be able to offer more sessions?

As counsellors, we need to focus on all types of endings as a key part of our skills, but sometimes little time is spent on this in training. Yet with every single client you have, there is going to be an ending – even in a simulated skills session at college. So I believe it's really important to look at this in depth. I hope that this chapter has helped you do that.

> **"**
>
> **It's a pictorial way of showing than ending doesn't mean 'never again' – more 'for now' – and it's an acknowledgement that life does go on after that ending.**
>
> **"**

Bibliography

BACP (2015) *Ethical Framework for the Counselling Professions*, BACP

Merry,T. and Lusty, B. (1993) What is Person-Centred Therapy?, Gale Centre Publications

Feltham, Colin, and Dryden, Windy (1993) *Dictionary of Counselling*, Whurr

Mearns, Dave, and Cooper, Mick (2005) *Relational Depth in Counselling and Psychotherapy*, Sage

Rogers, Carl (1942) *Counselling and Psychotherapy*, Houghton Miffin Co

Rogers, Carl (1959) 'A Theory of Therapy, Personality, and Interpersonal Relations, as Developed in the Client-Centered Framework', in Koch, Sigmund (ed.) *Psychology: A Study of a Science* (Volume 3), McGraw–Hill

Rogers, Carl (1961) *On Becoming a Person*, Constable

Tolan, Janet (2003) *Skills in Person-Centred Counselling & Psychotherapy*, Sage

Yalom, Irvin (1975) *The Theory and Practice of Group Psychotherapy*, Basic Books

Index

G

Gendlin, Eugene *89*

gentle challenge *71*

H

here-and-now *30, 96, 104, 105, 107, 109, 110, 112*

homeostasis *101*

I

Idiosyncratic *75, 78, 80, 83*

idiosyncratic empathy *78, 80, 82, 83, 97*

imagery *87, 89, 90, 91*

immediacy *93, 95, 96, 97, 98*

incongruence *69, 70, 71, 103, 106, 111*

incongruent *20, 102*

integrated *4, 22, 71, 81*

invite *3, 53, 54, 57, 97*

inviting *54*

J

Johari window *79*

L

listening *4, 19, 43, 53, 63, 66*

locus of evaluation *48*

M

metaphor *85, 87, 88, 89, 90, 91, 92, 121*

mirror *22, 79, 80, 82*

mirroring *21, 35*

moment of movement *30, 39, 48, 55, 56, 57, 70, 71*

movement *3, 22, 27, 30, 39, 48, 49, 55, 56, 57, 70, 71, 73, 112*

N

narrative *36, 37, 39, 46, 48, 61*

necessary and sufficient *15, 105*

non-directive *53*

non-maleficence *9*

non-verbal communication *31, 70, 77*

notes *13, 14, 20, 21, 43*

not-for-growth *79*

O

open questions *64*

organism *102*

organismic shift *30*

P

paraphrase *43, 45, 46, 48, 49, 57*

paraphrasing *29, 41, 43, 44, 45, 46, 47, 48, 49, 77*

PD *79*

PD groups *79*

perception *38, 45, 47, 77, 78*

personal development *79*

person-centred *9, 11, 15, 28, 53, 54, 61, 77, 81, 95, 119*

person-centred counselling *11, 28, 54*

placements *27*

planned ending *118, 120, 122*

power of silence *27, 31*

practice *3, 13, 27, 37, 66, 101, 115, 121, 122*

practise *12, 27, 31, 48, 57*

presence *46*

process *4, 29, 30, 36, 40, 48, 88, 91, 101, 102, 103, 105, 109, 111, 112, 116, 117, 118, 122*

process journal *88*

psychoanalytical *77*

psychodynamic *77*

psychological contact *77*

Q

question *5, 28, 37, 39, 61, 62, 63, 64, 65, 66, 81, 104, 105*

R

rapport *3, 17, 19, 20, 21, 22, 23, 31, 35, 37, 72*

rapport-building *19*

readiness to end *118, 119*

reflect *28, 30, 35, 36, 37, 38, 46, 63, 82, 89, 90, 91, 105, 106, 118*

reflection *29, 33, 35, 36, 37, 38, 39, 40, 54, 57, 65, 66, 77*

re-framing *90*

relational depth *3, 4, 22, 31, 57, 61, 91, 95, 98, 109*

rigidity to fluidity *15, 29, 70, 71*

Rogers, Carl *4, 15, 20, 31, 40, 43, 61, 77, 101, 127*

S

self-concept *73, 78, 79, 81, 106, 112, 117*

self-structure *79, 102*

seven stages of process *101, 109, 111, 112*

Made in the USA
Columbia, SC
11 July 2017